STRONG AND FREE

Canada and the New Sovereignty

FRANKLYN GRIFFITHS

Published in 1996 by
Stoddart Publishing Co. Limited
34 Lesmill Road
Toronto, Canada
M3B 2T6
Tel. (416) 445-3333
Fax (416) 445-5967

Revised and expanded version of an essay originally published in the
spring 1994 issue of *Canadian Foreign Policy*.

Stoddart Books are available for bulk purchase for sales promotions,
premiums, fundraising, and seminars. For details, contact the
Special Sales Department at the above address

Canadian Cataloguing in Publication Data

Griffiths, Franklyn, 1935–
Strong and free: Canada and the new sovereignty

ISBN 0-7737-5798-8

1. Popular culture – Canada.   2. Canada – Civilization –
American influences.   3. Canada – Civilization – Foreign influences.
4. Canada – Cultural policy.   I. Title.

FC95.4.G75 1996   306'.0971   C95-933267-7
F1021.2.G75 1996

Cover Design: the boy 100 & Tannice Goddard
Computer Graphics: Mary Bowness

Printed and bound in Canada

*Stoddart Publishing gratefully acknowledges the support of the
Canada Council and the Ontario Arts Council in the
development of writing and publishing in Canada.*

Contents

If we as a nation are concerned with the problem of defence, what, we may ask ourselves, are we defending? We are defending civilization, our share of it, our contribution to it. The things with which our inquiry deals are the elements which give civilization its character and its meaning. It would be paradoxical to defend something which we are unwilling to strengthen and enrich, and which we even allow to decline.

MASSEY COMMISSION, 1951

The tongueless man gets his land took.

CORNISH PROVERB

I

Recovering the Ground for Choice

Canadians, it seems, cannot agree. Fragmented and increasingly dispossessed by the globalization of economic life, disabled by deficits and debt of our own making, and now beset by an onrush of separatism and regionalism, we are coming apart. The Quebec referendum of October 30, 1995, was like a vivisection, as some performed an operation without anaesthetic on the identity of the rest of us. A *Maclean's*-CBC national poll released at the end of

1995 found Canada in the grip of unprecedented pessimism. Nearly one in three of us — and every second person in Quebec — shared the belief that the Canadian nation as we have known it will no longer exist by the end of the decade.[1] A country that is widely regarded as one of the most agreeable in the world is more and more convinced of its imminent destruction. As of early 1996, we believe we are losing it. And yet, we are almost certain to rally during the coming months in another effort to draw together.

There is a powerful desire among us to build on common ground, to recover the sense of shared enterprise. Despite our pessimism, we continue to be joined not only by our common identity but by a civilization of compassion and respect for diversity. But now that we have failed with the Meech Lake and Charlottetown accords, and witnessed near defeat in the Quebec referendum, we should not expect a fourth chance. This time, we have to get it right. Not only must we choose wisely together, but we must recover the ground for choice.

Canada is now so divided and in such difficult circumstances that brokerage politics alone will no longer suffice. Durable answers to our abundant economic, social, and constitutional dilemmas will continue to evade us as long as we fail to create a setting within the country that supports our ability to choose effectively for ourselves. Our problem is not one of particulars — a constitutional veto for Quebec, a pre-emptive federal referendum on unity, a deficit-reduction strategy at whatever level of government. Collective action on this plane, provided that adequate assent is cobbled together, can gain us needed time. But it will not take us far. When common ground is lacking among Canadians, brokerage politics lacks traction. To secure Canada is first and foremost to create a milieu within the country that strengthens and then sustains our ability to choose together. It is to enhance our capacity for autonomous choice.

Our condition is such that we should stand back from the compelling issues of the day. We need to take a hard look at what we are doing and are not doing to look after ourselves in a time of relentless change. Others have ventured much in this vein, most notably Richard Gwyn in his *Nationalism without Walls*.[2] My point of departure is to ask what it takes to make Canada secure. I am interested in those transformations of our situation that have overtaken conventional understandings of Canadian security. With Gwyn, I find that the challenge to our unity runs far beyond the dilemmas prompted by the desire of Quebeckers to be on their own. Defence of sovereignty is now of the essence in securing our country. Like nostalgia, sovereignty ain't what it used to be.

Canada's sovereignty is less and less the familiar matter of enforcing writ or title against foreign intruder, whether it be drug trafficker, illegal immigrant, terrorist, or uninvited American icebreaker. In essence, our problem is one of maintaining control over what happens *within* the national domain in an increasingly interdependent world. This is a world in which foreign indebtedness, ozone depletion, and the like pose ever more extreme challenges to our ability not only to look after ourselves but to decide for ourselves as a people. There is no way we can expect to deal effectively with disarray and disability within, if we define our problem without full reference to changes in our international environment. We are not in a position to wall Canada off from the effects of globalization, or to set ourselves up against all intrusion. Nor can we walk away from the effort to regulate what goes on between us and the world outside. Defence of sovereignty entails new and increasingly difficult choices in the international order that is taking shape in the wake of the Cold War.

Our sovereignty depends on our ability to make

sound choices in deciding when and how we are to be open to our international surround — and thus not only linked with it but vulnerable to it as well — or to be decoupled and protected from the world outside. In my view there is no great future for an approach to sovereignty that would attempt to insulate us from disruptive forces coming in from the external environment. But if we are to make the decisions required for Canada to remain an open and united country and also a sovereign state in an era of globalization, we need to be far more confident about who we are as a people. Managed openne — readiness to benefit from and adapt to an exterm.' setting that can also bring disruption and pain — requires a people who are together and who know it, because they see and feel it. As we lose the ability to give voice to feelings, ideas, and purposes that unite us, we stand to lose the ability to regulate and otherwise respond to international forces coming at us from abroad and tearing at us from within. In fact, we stand to lose control over our land. For Canada, defence of sovereignty comes down to our ability to nourish the processes that hold us together as a people with purposes and a destiny of our own on the continent of North America. Defence of sovereignty is, *au fond*, a matter of culture — political culture very much included.

The Massey Commission had it right more than four decades ago. In defending ourselves we are ultimately defending our civilization and our ability to make a contribution to world civilization.[3] In those days we were defending ourselves in a harsh Cold War setting where deterrence and the waging of war had far greater claim upon Canadian resources than defence of sovereignty. In the 1990s, sovereignty and its defence count for much more than war-fighting or deterrence in the security policy of a Canada that would hold together. Sovereignty now is not merely *a* but *the* critical element in Canada's security. It follows that a vibrant cultural life has abruptly acquired much greater importance in Canada's effort to be secure in the many meanings of the term. There is a sad commonality between 1951 and 1996: both years mark points in Canada's history when the capacity to make contributions to civilization had been allowed to decline in the midst of comparatively heavy defence spending. But while today we are faced with far greater and more unmanageable challenges to sovereignty than existed in 1951, it so happens that a plunge in the danger of war allows us to direct new resources to the defence of sovereignty, including culture, communications, and the recovery of ground for choice among Canadians.

Canada's sovereignty requirements have changed

in ways that demand a transfer of resources from defence to culture and communications. The state of our cultural life becomes a key variable in our security, in our survival as a people with the capacity to decide for ourselves in an interdependent world. Those who conceive of Canadian culture primarily in terms of cultural industries and employment potential will be asked to think again. Canadians will instead be invited to regard culture and communications as utterly fundamental in securing their country against internal as well as external threats to its well-being and cohesion.

II

Canada's Security Redefined

The idea of sovereignty is surrounded by all manner of clichés and conventions, to say nothing of stylish views about globalization and the demise of the nation-state. It's not easy to sort fact from fancy here. A discussion of concepts and realities is, however, essential if we are to understand Canada's sovereignty situation today. I propose to go into this area as lightly as possible in a series of short walks, rather than try the reader's patience with one long forced march. But before we take a step, I would be clear about two things.

Ours *is* a transitional era. In due course the nation-state, and with it national sovereignty, will almost certainly be replaced by new forms of association — by regional transnational entities, by metropolitan political economies at the subnational level.[1] The effects produced by such new "actors" will be based more on tasks performed than on territory held. But much of this reorganization is still in the future. Today, the shape of a new economic and political order is far from clear. Nor is it understood what role the nation-state will play in the formation of a new order. Accordingly, I believe it vital to protect the sovereignty of the Canadian people and the Canadian state until we begin to find better ways of looking after the populace and the natural environment within the domain called Canada. By sovereignty, again, I mean in the final analysis our capacity for autonomous choice, our ability as a people to work out our future for ourselves on our territory, even if this future should see us leave territorial sovereignty behind on a distant day.

Ours is also a transitional time in that the substance of security and the means of achieving it are both subject to change. Where means are concerned, we speak increasingly of common security. Lasting security is not to be had either at the expense of others or by unilateral action, when the sources of a deprivation (such as mass migration, currency fluctuation, or ozone depletion) are multilateral or global. As to substance, from being a notion centred on the use of military force in deterring and, if necessary, defeating an adversary or an opposing coalition, security now applies as well to all manner of non-military or civil threats, such as long-range airborne pollution or technological dependence. As distinct from nearly all military threats, civil challenges to the security of a state or a nation are challenges to national sovereignty — to the capacity of the state to enforce the law of the land, to maintain quality of life, and to the very ability to choose in an interdependent world. Though they may offer little or no threat of force, challenges to national sovereignty can still pose formidable threats to the security of a country like Canada. To some threats we may respond with unilateral action, which is by no means ruled out. More often we will react with measures of common security.

Our security situation is therefore quite novel today. Canada's long-standing requirements for military strength have largely been displaced by the need to deal with civil security threats. Defence of sovereignty becomes the main business in ensuring

Canada's security. It does so as the new century is upon us and, with it, new forms of association that ultimately may do better than the sovereign state in meeting basic human needs for prosperity, justice, and community.

THE CHANGING FACE OF SOVEREIGNTY

Let us make an unconventional distinction between two forms of sovereignty. One lies in the right of the state to exercise exclusive jurisdiction within a given space. Defined this way, sovereignty is essentially a legal notion (type 1 sovereignty). It connotes action to affirm Canada's boundaries against breaches of Canadian law from the outside. It is also the way most commentators understand the term.[2] But sovereignty can also be viewed as the condition of being supreme and free from external control in the governing of a given territory. The concept in this case is essentially political (type 2 sovereignty). Let us call this kind the new sovereignty. It suggests an effort, and not merely by the state, to deny and soften transboundary effects that reduce or threaten to reduce the quality of life, milieu, and government within Canada's borders. Illegal foreign fishing in Canada's offshore waters is a typical example of a type 1 sovereignty threat. Global warming, or Canadian indebtedness to foreign lenders, with the potential of either to constrain the quality of life, the environment, and the government alike, are representative of new sovereignty threats.

In the case of indebtedness, the problem stems from *Canadian* actions and inaction. Indeed, in 1996 the most pointed threat to the political and legal sovereignty of Canada is internal in nature: the determination of Quebec separatists to take the province out of Confederation. Whatever the sources of separatist sentiment in Quebec, Canada's difficulty in meeting the challenge or in finding a way of getting along without Quebec owes much to the fact that we in English-speaking Canada are ceasing to be the distinct society we once were. Due in no small measure to our failure to sustain our culture in an era of globalized communication, we are losing sight of who we are and the best we are capable of.

Leaving the question of Quebec for later, I suggest that Canada's sovereignty problem is undergoing fundamental change. The essence of the transformation is that type 1 challenges are being displaced with increasing rapidity by type 2 threats, without the Canadian people, or Canadian leaders, being fully aware of what's happening.

Type 1 threats come to mind almost reflexively in Canada when sovereignty is mentioned. Involving intentional violations of Canadian law, type 1 threats are also associated with opportunities for more or less focused responses by the government of Canada in policing its land, sea areas, and related airspace. Of all government agencies, it is the Department of National Defence that has by far the largest share of responsibility and budget for defence of sovereignty defined in type 1 terms. As to the new sovereignty, DND has little or nothing to offer in coping with transboundary processes that threaten the quality of life, the environment, or government in Canada. As a country, therefore, we are set up to deal primarily with old-style sovereignty problems with old-style hardware. At the same time, we are faced with the rapid rise of a novel sovereignty agenda, and we lack the knowledge and the means to act on it. Our priorities in making Canada secure are lagging far behind the times. They need to be changed.

National sovereignty is associated with nationalism and national self-determination. In different ways, all are having a bad press these days. Nationalist and separatist movements are widely viewed as the product of pathological impulses that give rise to civil and international wars, human rights violations, ethnic cleansing, and all manner of other enormities. Unbridled pursuit of national sovereignty also yields the vision of an increasingly chaotic international system with up to four hundred members, far too many of them incapable of responding properly to the needs of their people.[3] Further, it is true that a conventional or type 1 national sovereignty perspective, with its emphasis on borders and policing, is out of keeping with the practicalities of environmental protection and conservation — for example, in the abatement of long-range air-borne pollution or the protection of fish stocks that straddle contiguous waters of two or more states. And, finally, we have the thought that there's something mean-spirited and inward-looking about a live concern for national sovereignty when other more generous impulses and concepts are available to inspire more cooperative, caring, and just foreign behaviour that promises to address global inequalities. In short, sovereignty does have its problems, and it needs to be viewed critically.

Where Canada in particular is concerned, the word sovereignty evokes images of domination by the United States. It suggests nationalist feelings of resentment. Potent rushes of Canadian opinion in defence of sovereignty have been prompted by American violations of Canadian jurisdiction in the waters of the Arctic Archipelago in connection with the voyages of the SS *Manhattan* in 1969–70 and the *Polar Sea* in 1985.[4] Among Canada's Arctic Aboriginal peoples, however, the appeal of national sovereignty is less impressive, given the High Arctic Exiles' experience as pawns in the defence of sovereignty against the United States after 1952.[5] Add the perennial voicing of concern to safeguard culture against corrosive influence from south of the border, and it could be said that defence of sovereignty is really about Canada–U.S. relations and not much else. This would be a parochial view, and an inaccurate one, too. The most recent surge of Canadian support for sovereignty came with the seizure of the Spanish trawler, the *Estai*, and the ensuing row with the European Union in 1995. More important, the challenges of the new sovereignty go well beyond transboundary relations in North America alone.[6]

Whether or not they are confronted within by communities who would drop out in pursuit of national self-determination, nation-states everywhere are besieged from without by processes of globalization that could one day deny the very possibility of governance at the national level. As information, images, and money flow with ever greater velocity through ever more integrated global communications networks, national governments are being deprived of the ability to meet public expectations of good economic management and, indeed, good government as such. Exchange and interest rates, technological innovation, and intrafirm transfers are all escaping national control, leaving the state less sovereign in its territory even as title to land and water remains absolutely secure. In no way is Canada exempt from such considerations, which apply equally well to globalization of the environment and to environmental protection. Nor is Canada exempt from still other travails of the state that would govern in a shrinking world.

As governments are driven to negotiate ever more intimate forms of cooperation in arrangements such as the North American Free Trade Agreement, others stand to gain a greater say in a country's internal affairs — for example, on the propriety of domestic subsidies, food marketing boards, or regulations governing advertising in magazines.[7] Such arrangements are in no way inconsistent with type 1 sovereignty, which accords the state unquestioned authority to enter into agreements limiting its freedom of action. But like much of what we are talking about here, intimate interstate collaboration does pose a frontal challenge to type 2 sovereignty. The more such collaboration we have, the more it tears at the social cohesion and national identity of Canadians. It widens divisions within society, and between the state and those who find their principal loyalty at the local, provincial, or global level.

Some globalists — take William Thorsell, for

example — go so far as to welcome the decline of sovereignty. They see a benefit to Canada, somehow, in the hemorrhaging of sovereignty to stateless transnational corporations. A willing surrender of sovereignty is seemingly favoured so that we can immerse ourselves in the "emerging world culture of music, film, fashion, design and television that easily transcends national boundaries and regulation."[8] Canadians, however, tend to be internationalists, not globalists. They favour institution-building and cooperation among nation-states, not those forces that would obliterate the nation-state. Until something demonstrably superior to national sovereignty comes along, Canadians will surely remain internationalists and act accordingly. To do otherwise would be to set ourselves up for takeover.

Well beyond globalization and the piercing and lowering of today's borders, there lies the prospect of international transformations that could effectively marginalize the nation-state. As a trend-spotter, Peter Drucker emphasizes the growth of transnational institutions, regionalism, and what he terms tribalism.[9] More apposite, perhaps, is the vision of a new medievalism or world order without the prominent territorially based actors we have today.[10] It could be that the "real decision-making powers of the future . . . will be transnational companies in alliance with city-regional governments."[11] The trick in making the transition to such a world will be to preserve Canada's autonomy, sense of community, and identity even as we begin to explore ways of moving beyond the nation-state as our primary political attachment.

Selective defence of sovereignty is therefore absolutely essential for Canada's security and, indeed, its survival. As we begin to test our ability to create new economic and political structures based on information, communications, technology, and a sustaining culture, the enduring objective in defending Canadian sovereignty cannot be either to keep the unwanted out or to persist as we are within. Our aim must be to gain the time required to invent and make use of new forms for survival in the world that is already upon us. Defence of sovereignty, type 2 principally, is now the chief task of Canadian security policy. By the same token, as distinctions between foreign and internal affairs are being wiped out, Canada's prime concern today must be security writ large, not just "foreign" policy and "defence" policy.

III

Security and the New Sovereignty

Canada's need to lift sovereignty to the top of its security priorities is not primarily the result of the end of the Cold War. The revolutionary forces that are transforming our country, its international surround, and our security requirements run far deeper than the challenges of communism or its collapse. The end of the Cold War is nevertheless liberating. It frees up imagination and resources at a time when we need urgently to redefine what security means to

us and how best to achieve it. It enables us to demilitarize our understanding of security and of ways
to seek it. It allows us to do the same for sovereignty.

On an unamended military-technical understanding of security, the end of the Cold War all but
removes the danger of direct attack upon Canada
and North America. As to the prospect of a major
power land war breaking out in Europe without
much warning and with serious consequences for
Canada's security, it's gone. What then is left for the
Canadian Forces? Two things: defence of sovereignty,
and participation in United Nations, North Atlantic
Treaty Organization, and ad hoc peacekeeping forces.
Peacekeeping, however, is discretionary for Canada.
We are neither compelled nor obliged to do it. There
is nothing to stop us from finding ways of transferring
to overseas development assistance all the resources
now committed to peacekeeping, should we wish to
do so. But we *do* have to defend directly against those
who would violate Canadian law or challenge
Canadian jurisdiction from abroad. There is no
choice. A government that threw up its hands and
said it was leaving the field to terrorists, drug smugglers, and the like would be crucified. In addition,
the Canadian government must be able to demon-
strate effective occupancy of this vast country by
having some ability to respond to events anywhere on

land, in the air, and out to 200 miles offshore on three oceans.

Viewed only in military terms, the end of the Cold War and the greatly diminished likelihood of coalition warfare among major powers urge upon us a fundamental restructuring of defence priorities. The change that is required would see defence of type 1 sovereignty move to primacy of place among the military missions of the Canadian Forces. By no means would this change exclude international operations. Plenty of capability would remain for this kind of activity, especially if type 1 sovereignty tasks were handled by the Canadian Forces in closer cooperation with other government departments such as the Royal Canadian Mounted Police and Fisheries and Oceans. Nevertheless, prevailing views on what is fit and proper for the use of armed force in distant areas by Canada would be substantially altered. Debt and deficit enter the picture here. No longer able to afford defence capabilities enabling us to respond in a full range of contingencies, we would make a choice rather than nickel and dime the Canadian Forces into disability. We would identify a niche and fill it. War-fighting missions would be out. Constabulary or police-type operations would be in and would call for action at the low-intensity end of the spectrum of possible uses of force. Configuring our forces for constabulary action, we would be well on the way to acknowledging the need to demilitarize our approach to Canada's security: the Canadian Forces would become committed primarily to policing operations against essentially non-military or civil threats to Canadian sovereignty. In terms of budget and procurement, a Canadian interest in military capabilities for defence of type 1 sovereignty could go well with a selective approach to international peacekeeping that favoured our aptitude for police action, and that left to others the opportunity for heavy coercion.

The views being advanced here for Canadian defence are not new. They were articulated with great force in the *Canada 21* report that appeared early in 1994.[1] But the Canadian government has not so far been clearly swayed by the case for the constabulary principle. In fact, the defence department has been able to persist in the effort to acquire a replacement submarine fleet.[2] Hard choices are being avoided in the midst of continuing budget cuts that have seen annual defence spending decline from $12.4 to $9.9 billion in the period since 1992. Following parliamentary hearings and an official review of defence, the department issued a white paper in December 1994 which sought to continue with business as usual while also bowing to the government's enlarged commitment to peacekeeping. Somehow we are to muster multipurpose combat-capable forces allowing us "to fight 'alongside the best, against the best.'"[3] This course of action, which favours coalition warfare and peace enforcement as primary missions, will surely be proven unworkable. Far better that we face up to the realities of our financial and security situation, opt for peacekeeping, and reallocate resources without delay to meet the civil as well as the military challenges of the new sovereignty.

The end of the Cold War, and of attendant concerns over the danger and deterrence of major power warfare, has also contributed to the appearance of new thinking, in Canada as elsewhere, about international security per se.[4] Standard military considerations continue to figure in the discussion, but gradually they are being offset by an awareness of the uses of political reassurance, as distinct from the balancing of force, in producing safety. More important in the long term, international security discourse is being widened to include economic, environmental, demographic, and other dimensions reaching down to security of the person. Further, security is more often viewed not so much in national as in global terms, with threats to the human condition posed by population growth or global warming. The combined effect of these developments is to encourage the demilitarization of thinking about security. First signs of official conversion to this line of thought in Canada are to be had in the government response, issued by the Department of Foreign Affairs and International Trade in February 1995, to the parliamentary reappraisal of foreign policy that was conducted in tandem with the defence review. The government statement refers, for example, to the need for a "broader concept of security, and to the increased significance of global environmental, demographic and other threats." It further agrees with the need for selectivity in Canada's peacekeeping involvement, but then joins with Defence in undertaking to avoid "undue fine-tuning" of the Canadian Forces.[5] Clearly, the government is not of a single mind in defining and responding to Canada's changed security environment. An opening has been achieved for incorporating new thinking about security and, sooner or later, sovereignty into public policies that are adapted to the realities of Canada's situation.

In the notion of common security, it is recognized that international and national security are inseparable. Given a setting of globalization and interdependence, one state cannot gain lasting military, economic, environmental, or other security at the expense of another. By the same token, self-help and opposed-forces behaviour are unable to meet the requirements of security in a shrinking world where action in common is increasingly a precondition for success in resolving threats to any one state. For example, if Russia dumps nuclear waste materials at sea today and is the inheritor of catastrophic Soviet military and civilian dumping practices in Arctic waters, the contamination will affect Canada's environment and can be dealt with only through collective action.[6] A practice and a discourse of common security can thus be seen as drawing attention to non-military dimensions of international security, and to the limits of military means of achieving it. Both in substance and in regard to means, there is an overlap between common security and the new sovereignty.

In acting for common security and for the new sovereignty, we would find ourselves relying largely on non-military means to deal with non-military threats to security. To be sure, there is a difference of standpoint. A common security perspective inclines us to quit the perspective of the nation-state and to consider cooperative action for the common good in conditions of interdependence — indeed, planetary interdependence. A new sovereignty perspective, on the other hand, remains anchored in the national view, but also allows that non-military threats to quality of life, the environment, and governance may often be met only by action in concert with others — as, for instance, in dealing with long-range transport of pollutants, with mass migrations, and with overfishing in international waters adjacent to the national domain. As goals and as activities, common security and the new sovereignty are sufficiently alike for us to say they are both expressions of security. Both can gain new prominence in Canada's security policy only as events oblige us to surrender our long-standing preoccupation with the demands of alliance and collective action to prevent a third world war. But there is another difference.

The new sovereignty is concerned with quality of government in a world of globalization and transboundary processes that subvert the very ability to govern. Type 1 threats to sovereignty do not seem likely to assume proportions that will challenge the capacity of the Canadian state to govern for the Canadian people. But type 2 threats are already doing just this and promise to aggravate in the years ahead. In keeping with a common security perspective, we should find ways of joining with other countries to address new sovereignty threats at source — for example, through participation in United Nations peacekeeping operations, by encouraging international trading practices that make for higher employment in countries that otherwise might produce large numbers of migrants, or by providing technologies that reduce the emission of greenhouse gasses from coal-fired generating stations. But what good is the contribution to common security if all along we are incorporating others' interests ever more directly into the definition of our own interests? if others' views of their interests remain unchanged while we lose the capacity to act on the situation at home and abroad as we see it? The point here is that globalization can gradually deprive the Canadian state and the Canadian people of the capacity for good government — indeed, the capacity to make autonomous choices as such — no matter how well we do on behalf of common security and common responses to global challenges.

The common security agenda does not have much room for problems of governance within the nation-state. This restriction is quintessentially the problem of the new sovereignty, which may require self-help and self-reliance as well as action in concert with others. As a rule of thumb, it seems advisable to opt for collaboration rather than unilateral action when cost considerations are roughly equal, and when sovereignty and collective security objectives can both be met in a given international undertaking.

But in the final analysis, the prime threat to Canada's security and sovereignty is not armed attack, pollution, proliferation of means of mass destruction, overpopulation, pestilence, or other dangers that may be met through international cooperation in the long haul. It is the erosion of our ability to choose for ourselves, in the here and now. In this we have further reason to regard defence of sovereignty as the uppermost consideration in Canadian security policy today.

SOVEREIGNTY, CIVILITY, CULTURE

How then are we to sustain Canada's capacity for autonomous choice in an era of globalization? We need to devise better ways of bringing professional expertise and political leadership together in evaluating the diverse threats to Canadian sovereignty, in assigning priorities among them, and in developing options for policy. We need to assign intellectual and political resources to the task of inventing new forms of association that may meet the varied needs of our people as the nation-state is marginalized. We also need to find ways of changing our thinking about security and about sovereignty, as inevitably it is subject to erosion in the years ahead. Most important, there is the need within Canada to foster what may be called enabling background conditions for choice.

Our most critical task is not to get Ottawa properly motivated and organized to solve problems itself, or to change public thinking on this or that question. It is to nourish a milieu that is conducive to Canadians seeing things and defining things for ourselves in ways that work for us. As I envisage it, such a milieu will have two interrelated dimensions, the political and the cultural. To be able to look after ourselves as a people, we need first to affirm Canada's political culture of civility. In turn, for civility to thrive, we must look anew to the needs of popular culture and communications in this country.

If there is one word that captures the essence of what Canada is about, and of what we would encourage elsewhere, it is civility. I mean by civility an attitude of respect and consideration in dealings among private citizens, in relations between state and society, and in the relations of individuals and the state to the natural environment and to other peoples.[7] We in Canada aim for greater civility in this world, whether it be through United Nations peacekeeping, overseas development assistance, avoidance of trade wars through GATT, support for human rights, an open immigration policy, or through international environmental protection. We strive for greater civility because we know from our own experience that it is a precondition for choices that all can live with. The experience of Canada's Aboriginal peoples tells us as well that there is no substitute for attitudes of respect and consideration in making choices that affect the natural environment. Indeed, the rest of us have much to learn from Aboriginal peoples about civilization and civilized behaviour on a planet with finite carrying capacity.

The notion of civility being advanced here has little to do with politeness or with instructing others on how to behave. On the contrary, it stresses the ability to consider as well as hear what others are saying, *and* what the natural environment may be communicating to us. As such, it assists Canadians in making not only choices, but hard choices all can live with in deciding where to be open and where closed to the world outside. This it does by favouring consensus in the making of decisions, and cohesion in support of decisions once taken. In short, a culture of civility makes for a people who are together politically. Conversely, without civility, as throughout the former Yugoslavia, and without the ability to work things out, we risk the descent into chaos and violence.

A live culture of civility is a precondition for sovereignty understood as autonomy of choice, including choices that add up to contributions to civilization. Autonomy is furthered when the frame-

a likelier danger – US radical individualis

work of choice is a civil one that neither excludes nor marginalizes, that finds ways of talking through to unity of purpose. As to civilization, how better might Canada contribute to civilization than by encouraging awareness and acceptance of civility as a norm of international behaviour? Could it also be that civility is preferable to security as a global aim, given the simplicity of the idea of civility and the inordinate complexity of a multidimensional conception of security as a guide to behaviour? And all the while, should we not seek an international setting that is consistent with our own basic values, with a desire to maintain autonomy of choice by encouraging civility at home and abroad?

So the question of sovereignty as autonomous choice becomes in part a question of maintaining and invigorating a culture of civility within Canada. As pointed out in the report of the Public Policy Forum, *Making Government Work*, there is much that can readily be done to reduce the extraordinary alienation of Canadians from their government by making the state more responsive to society.[8] My concern, however, is rather more with society. Since the Massey Commission reported, civility has declined in this country. Consideration and mutual respect have been eroded in many walks of life, in public affairs as in relations between Quebec and the rest of Canada. In the loss of civility we see the fracturing effects on Canadian society of globalization and, in the past decade, of government action that not only has been blind to the mounting challenge of the new sovereignty but also has sided with globalization in the name of enhanced Canadian competitiveness. It is time to turn things around.

A political culture of civility is embedded in and depends upon the shared experience of participation in a national culture. Take the latter away or dilute it with global culture, and the practice of civility gives way more readily under the stress of social change. Canadian intolerance of immigration, for example, seems to have grown not so much from economic stress as from a deeper "cultural insecurity — the fear that an ill-defined Canadian way of life is disappearing."[9] Civility comes easier when people know one another, when they see they have something in common, when in images and sound and print they freely experience and voice what joins them. The vital thing here is not culture understood in terms of product — television programs, films, sports events, books, concerts, paintings — but the potential for these artifacts to knit large numbers of people together in experiencing their own particular reality or an associated reality they had not known of. The more vital Canada's cultural life, the greater the civility among Canadians, the stronger the basis for autonomous choice, and the more assured the sovereignty of the country in defining its own future.

In sum, a conception of Canada's security that is adapted to the contemporary revolution in human affairs is one that elevates defence of the new sovereignty to primacy of place over all other security tasks. Effective defence of sovereignty is inconceivable without a supporting culture of civility and, beyond that, a vigorous cultural life on which everything Canadian ultimately depends. Without our fully understanding it, the security value of Canadian cultural life has been growing for many years. We need to understand this connection now, and to act on it. We also need to appreciate that in nurturing the culture and communications of Canada we are making a contribution to common security. As with the extinction of species, the extinction of cultures is detrimental to the security of humankind. As monoculture makes farming vulnerable to sudden change of conditions, cultural homogeneity that stems from globalization runs counter to humanity's interest in survival. As we respond to unprecedented circumstances, we need to be able to draw on as varied a repertoire of cultures as possible. Canadian sovereignty ultimately goes hand in hand with common security.

IV

Threats to Canadian Sovereignty

A fully substantiated and ranked list of threats to Canadian sovereignty as they may be expected to evolve over the next few years is more than can be produced in a short book. We may, however, survey key parts of the field in scrutinizing the proposition that the new sovereignty poses the overriding challenge for those who would make Canada secure. Given a sense of the combined threat we face in the years ahead, we should be in a position to consider just what Canada and Canadians need to do on behalf of sovereignty now.

TYPE 1 THREATS

Among threats to Canadian sovereignty defined essentially in legal terms are those entailing, first, challenges to Canada's title, as in the waters of the Arctic Archipelago, in the Beaufort Sea, and in the Dixon Entrance. Next we have actions involving illegal entry into areas of Canadian jurisdiction by officials or other agents of foreign states, including submarine commanders, intelligence officers, and air-craft pilots. Third, unlawful entry of private persons, such as illegal immigrants, international terrorists, and drug traffickers. And, fourth, illicit activity within Canada by private persons who may have entered legally, such as captains of vessels that fish illegally in or pollute Canadian waters, private pilots in violation of air traffic control regulations, or industrial spies. Canadians may be, and in fact often are, highly exercised by certain of these violations, especially those that involve terrorist activities, drug smuggling, and immigration. But in none of them can we see a danger that amounts to a threat to Canada's survival. Nor can we readily envisage any one of them getting so far out of hand as to threaten our survival in the course of the first decade into the next century. Nevertheless, when it comes to sovereignty, this is where most of the live concern of Canadians is currently to be found.

Consider, for example, illegal immigration, which administrators sometimes refer to as irregular migration.[1] In this case the perception has been growing among Canadians that Canada's laws are being broken and bent from the outside.[2] Though the number of irregulars who enter by avoiding Canada's determination system appears to be small, the public perception of abuse and illegality calls almost for the raising of walls, thereby potentially affecting Canada's status as an immigration country with a goal of 250,000 entrants annually. The issue here is a serious one for confidence in government, for quality of life, and for civility in this country.

As to the full extent of the immigration problem that might one day face Canada, it would seem ultimately to consist of increasing numbers of boat people landing surreptitiously on Canadian shores, and of mass appearances of refugee claimants at airports and at border crossings from the United States. In fact, the outlook for later in the next century is one of ever larger mass migrations prompted by war, environmental degradation, trade restrictions, population growth, famine, and human rights violations by governments in impoverished countries.[3] Canada will not be exempted from these mass movements. But if our concern is with the likelihood of any great surge in the number of irregular migrants into Canada by the turn of the next century, it does not seem to be great. This reading of the immigration or migration issue suggests that the threat is neither substantial now nor likely to balloon quickly. More or less the same could be said of other type 1 challenges to Canadian sovereignty. Consider the Arctic.

Canada's exclusive jurisdiction in the Arctic is challenged explicitly by the United States and tacitly by other maritime states. Canada's Arctic lands are not at issue here. The key problem is with the status of the Northwest Passage or the waters of the Arctic Archipelago.[4] These the United States regards as constituting an international strait, which connects two high seas areas and through which all states have virtually unconstrained rights of transit. For Canada, these waters are internal and are not open to foreign transit except with prior Canadian permission sought and obtained. A Canada–U.S. agreement of January 1988 shelved the dispute, as it concerned transit by American surface vessels, notably icebreakers.[5] But nothing was said about American nuclear-powered attack submarines, which could be continuing to transit the Archipelago on missions to and from the Arctic Ocean today.[6]

The threat here is that American nuclear submarines, in repeated and unchallenged transits, may be creating an international practice that strengthens the U.S. claim that the waters in question are in law an international strait. Further, the risk of accident befalling a nuclear submarine is surely greater in constricted ice-infested waters than in the ice-covered sea. Were a nuclear submarine to be disabled under the ice in the Archipelago, the U.S. government would proceed to its rescue immediately and without concern for diplomatic niceties. Canada would find itself in the awkward position of granting permission, which had not been sought, for an American rescue effort to reach a submarine that ought not to have been there in the first place. Add the potential for dispersal of radioactive material in an accident, and we have a combined threat to the environment, to Canada's occupancy of disputed waters, and to the Canadian claim of exclusive jurisdiction.

The Department of National Defence has for years been planning to deploy acoustic sensors at certain choke points in the Archipelago, in order to monitor subsurface use of Canadian waters. An Arctic Subsurface Surveillance System is still in the Defence program, but it is sidelined. A letter in mid-1995 from the minister's senior adviser reported that an operationally acceptable and cost-effective system continued to be sought.[7] And now the minister has cited cost considerations in declaring that while the need "remains, there is at present no intention to deploy a system."[7]

Similar to illegal immigration, then, the threat to Canada's Arctic sovereignty is one in which potentially disastrous consequences — in this instance for the environment — are offset by a low probability that the worst will occur within the next several years. The judgment of low probability is derived from the overall safety record of U.S. nuclear submarines, and from the consideration that Arctic patrols by these American vessels could very well become less frequent, if they haven't already, owing to the end of the Cold War. At the same time, Canada's Arctic sovereignty could well be subject to piecemeal erosion as a consequence of continuing American transits. A government that is truly committed to Arctic sovereignty should find a way to deploy an Arctic Subsurface Surveillance System.

Making our way through a range of type 1 threats to Canadian sovereignty, we seem likely to judge them all manageable to one degree or another in the near to mid term. I am thinking of international terrorism, drug trafficking and money laundering, foreign military and political intelligence-gathering in Canada, economic espionage by foreign governments and private entities, foreign penetration of counter-part ethnic communities in Canada, military incursions into Canadian space, illegal fishing[8] or dumping of pollutants into Canadian waters, and so on. In none of these matters will Canada's security, to say nothing of Canada's survival as a country, be exposed to massive and effective challenges. In all such matters the potential for the Canadian people to become agitated is nevertheless substantial. The government of Canada must, and ordinarily does, manage its type 1 sovereignty agenda with care. But there is also a need for Canadians to educate themselves and to act on a set of less familiar sovereignty problems.

NEW SOVEREIGNTY THREATS

At issue here are boundary-crossing phenomena and processes that can and do degrade the quality of life, the environment, and government within Canada if left unmet. Threats to sovereignty that imperil our ability to determine our own future do not violate our title, our jurisdiction, or our specific Canadian legislation. But debilitation of our capacity for choice does subvert our ability to defend our title and our jurisdiction. Four sets of challenges are raised by the new sovereignty. First, we have human-originated physical effects that defy unilateral reaction, as with global warming, ozone depletion, acid rain, Arctic haze, and the emergence of new communicable diseases. Second, we have purposive human activity that yields effects which are destructive of political sovereignty but cannot be considered unlawful or illegitimate, as with the implications of globalization for Canada's ability to control interest rates and otherwise to conduct an economic policy tailored to a Canadian view of Canadian needs; with foreign retaliation in response to perceived Canadian environmental degradation such as occurs in response to clear-cutting in British Columbia; with the effects of the anti-fur movement in Europe on Aboriginal ways of life in Canada's North; or with foreign overfishing of straddling stocks in international waters adjacent to the 200-mile Canadian fisheries zone. Third, we are faced with transboundary effects of action and inaction on the part of Canadians, as with technological dependence, the erosion of Canadian culture, or with Canadian foreign indebtedness and its many consequences for Canadian choice. Finally and most urgently, we have the indigenous danger of breakup arising from separatist sentiment in Quebec. Quebec separatism is obviously a frontal challenge to type 1 sovereignty, but it is treated here as a new sovereignty issue owing to its disabling effects on Canada, whether or not separation occurs. Many of the phenomena gathered here are capable of doing deeper and more lasting damage to the quality of life, physical milieu, and government in Canada than any of the type 1 threats we might consider. Global warming and ozone depletion could well fall into this category.[9] Quebec separatism surely does.

In separatism and the growth of regionalism, we have an expression not only of the Canadian but of the global condition. Sooner or later, most nation-states are destined to encounter a situation not unlike ours. Whereas one in three Canadians now anticipate the destruction of their country by the year 2000, one in three Americans already expect that the United States will have broken up by 2095.[10] The Canadian condition is one of dwindling commitment to the nation in the nation-state, coupled with mounting frustration at the inability of the state in the nation-state to produce prosperity and equity. A sensible approach in the circumstances is one that urges the affirmation of national sovereignty defined in terms of autonomous choice, as well as a readiness to explore new forms of association that yield more agreeable choices. We should, however, defer consideration of what needs to be done for Canadian unity until we have a clearer understanding of the new sovereignty and its requirements.

Aside from what has already been said about

globalization and the constraints it imposes on the conduct of national economic policy by the state, other aspects of the problem warrant attention.[11] As finance, production, and trade break free of territorial constraints and become not only transnational but global in scope and force, a world economic system begins to take shape. It is in the nature of a system that it shapes the behaviour of units or nation-states within, units that also perform global functions such as national programs for education, science, and technological innovation that help maintain the system writ large. Today's industrial or post-industrial restructuring is an example: it has truly global force and readily invokes the supporting resources of the state. The point here is not only that the Canadian state is channelled and constricted by the global economic system in its choice of national economic options and instruments, but that the government of Canada is itself becoming an agent of globalization. The state faces outwards increasingly as it loses control over the national economy. Inevitably the state answers somewhat less to the people of Canada, and somewhat more to transnational private actors such as banks, bond raters, currency traders, and international financial institutions. In a word, the Canadian state is in the process of being turned around.

In the progressive decoupling of the state from the nation in matters of political economy, a terminal threat to national sovereignty comes into view. Not only does the state lose the capacity to shape the economic and social life of the country but it loses interest. Though the threat in this case will almost certainly not be realized in full over the coming decade, the lead times required to institute alternative structures of governance are so great that Canadian sovereignty must be considered an endangered species. By the same token, the state today does retain some ability to shield and strengthen the Canadian capacity for choice. It can buy time for Canadians to move forward into alternative social and political arrangements that eventually may have little to do with national sovereignty. In particular, there is nothing to prevent the federal government from acting now to sustain a vigorous cultural life in Canada, and to contain the threat of global and especially American culture to Canada's ability to choose for itself.

As argued earlier, the capacity for autonomous choice is dependent on a practice of civility, which in turn relies on the shared experience of participation in a wider culture centred on the arts, information, and entertainment. The field of view can for a moment be enlarged to include research in the sciences and the humanities. In an era when the threat to sovereignty acquires radically new qualities, knowledge becomes increasingly vital in Canada's ability to set its own policy agenda. We need to be able to define our situation for ourselves, to define our own policy options, and to communicate among ourselves on these matters in ways that improve the likelihood of consensus. To accept deficiencies here is to accept threats that go to the heart of Canada's ability to decide for itself.

But my concern in this book is not so much with expert contributions to the communications process or with high culture. It is with the potential benefits of popular culture and the mass media in regaining the ground for choice. For these benefits to be obtained, the Canadian people need to experience themselves, their country, and the world around in newscasts and current affairs programs, in television and radio programs, in movies and books produced by Canadians, and not by others for foreign markets. Without such offerings, widely shared understandings of the situations we face, and of collective responses to them, are hard to conceive. Nor could there be reliable backing for policy once the country's agenda was set. In 1996 Canadians find themselves in an increasingly fractious country battered by recession and global economic restructuring, divided along regional lines, lacking in potent national systems of communication, and with a badly shaken government that must now repair damage done to the sense of common enterprise.

Unusual disarray and diminishing civility in our public affairs are connected at some level with processes occurring in our cultural life. In the erosion of federal support for the cultural sector, especially since the late 1980s, we have a self-inflicted wound that threatens not only our unity but our capacity for choice. Federal support is necessary if Canadians are to benefit from the shared experience of Canadian images, thought, and preferences in a Canadian marketplace where the United States would otherwise eliminate most competition by virtue of economies of scale and amortization of cost in its own market.

To be specific, reductions in capital cost allowances on federal tax have choked private investment in film and television shows for some years now.[12] Postal rates have increased for publications, raising costs to buyers, with predictable effects on sales. As well, the goods and services tax was applied to books, magazines, and newspapers despite prior exemption of such materials from federal sales tax. A couple of years ago, forward budgeting for the CBC could have left the corporation with operating funds in 1997–98 that were 10 percent higher than in 1984–85, inflation notwithstanding. Now the CBC has been obliged to absorb multimillion dollar cuts even before the report of the task force struck in 1995 to review the mandates of Canada's three national film, video, and broadcast institutions.[13] Leaving aside federal support for the cultural sector considered but forgone in recent years, we may conclude that the interest of the state in a vigorous and independent cultural life has diminished substantially at a time when reinforcement of the capacity for choice has become the uppermost requirement in making Canada secure. By one count, total federal spending in current dollars for the cultural sector increased 3.7 percent between 1984–85 and 1991–92, whereas spending for defence increased 38.6 percent in the same period.[14] In these numbers we have stark evidence of Canada's need to correct its approach to sovereignty and security by lending powerful new support to culture and communications.

As of early 1996, a moment of truth is approaching. At issue is the long-awaited report of the task force, headed by Pierre Juneau, to review the mandates of the CBC, the National Film Board, and Telefilm Canada.[15] A lengthy technical document that ends with 95 recommendations, the Juneau report calls for fundamental change in the programming, administration, and funding of all three instiutions so as to make them more responsive to the cultural needs of Canadian citizens. Though immediately drawn into a cloud of controversy over its recommendations of a telecommunications tax to fund the CBC, the enduring value of the report will surely shine through. Juneau and his colleagues have succeeded in developing actionable alternatives to those who would have governments withdraw and give market forces full sway over a small and fragmented audience that borders on the most dynamic entertainment and communications market in the world. Their report should figure prominently in the coming struggle to reaffirm the common purpose of Canadians.

We are not dealing here with "cultural industries" to be deregulated, downsized, privatized, or left to the whim of North American "'consumer sovereignty' as our primary organizing principle."[16] In broadcasting, film, and video, and also in publishing and the arts we have the lifeblood of Canada. In the absence of a sustained civilization of our own, Canadians — Quebeckers included — risk becoming atomized seekers of gratification and identity south of the border and elsewhere. We risk ending up with defence forces aspiring vainly to fight "alongside the best," and with a sorely diminished country, or no country, left to defend.

In sum, the calculus of Canadian sovereignty is

now sufficiently altered for us to say it has been transformed. The new sovereignty agenda displaces military understandings of security and type 1 sovereignty in the effort to secure our country. The essence of our task is to protect not against this or that threat or combination of challenges, but to protect the capacity for choice itself. To succeed, we must make it a priority to strengthen the civilization that joins us. Consistent with the transition from labour and hardware to knowledge and software in the functioning of advanced societies, it may also be said that our security increasingly depends on knowledge and intelligence, as distinct from equipment and personnel. Finally, in responding to the threatened breakup of the country, we have no choice but to begin the work of designing alternative forms of association that meet the diverse needs for community and civility in the common space now called Canada.

V

What Is to Be Done?

The transformation in Canada's security situation has produced a significant mismatch between available capabilities and new requirements for the defence of sovereignty as the country's prime security task. There is a lack of fit between the present configuration of the Canadian Forces for war-fighting and the comparatively modest capabilities needed to perform type 1 sovereignty tasks and international constabulary missions. A second mismatch is to be seen in the near complete inability of the Canadian Forces to respond to type 2 sovereignty imperatives. As well, certain preconditions for cost-effective action in defence of sovereignty are not met. For example, we lack an integrated evaluation process within government which would make it possible to assess varied dangers to sovereignty, to assign priority among them, and to facilitate choice among common security and unilateral responses available to Canada. And then there is the major mismatch in the way we allocate funds to make ourselves secure. The defence share of expenditure is wholly excessive relative to our need to underwrite the capacity for collective choice. We are unlikely to do our best for national unity in the months and years ahead if we fail to recognize the need for a transfer of funds in support of culture and communications. None of these matters need be considered in detail here. It is important, however, to be clear about key directions for the defence of Canadian sovereignty now and into the next century.

THE CANADIAN FORCES CONFIGURED FOR SOVEREIGNTY

The Canadian Forces in 1996 are structured "to protect Canada, contribute to world peace, and protect Canadian interests abroad."[1] These broad objectives lead to a lengthy list of further purposes. They are "to defend Canada by protecting Canada's national territory and jurisdictional areas, helping civil authorities protect and sustain national interests, and assisting in national emergencies; to cooperate with the United States in protecting North America and promoting Arctic and Western hemispheric security; and to contribute to international security by participating in the full range of multilateral operations through the United Nations, NATO, other regional organizations, or coalitions of like-minded countries; supporting humanitarian relief efforts and restoration of conflict-devastated areas; and participating in arms control and other confidence-building measures."[2] In the phrase "full range of multilateral operations," this mission statement for the Canadian Forces mandates an open-ended capability and expenditure requirement for heavy armour and advanced naval and air power for use against the submarines, bombers, fighter aircraft, and artillery and armoured formations of a formidable adversary or opposing coalition. Hard choices are avoided. As stated by the *Canada 21* report in words that remain fully relevant today:

> The choice before Canadians is not between forces that could defend Canada against military attack and those that could not. Rather, the choice is between, on the one hand,

making the decisions that will allow Canada to
play a leading role in the new era of common
security, and on the other, continuing with
present policies which both make that option
increasingly difficult, and at the same time,
maintain an assortment of military capabilities
too limited to be effective for any meaningful
purpose. Only a much larger defence budget
could solve this dilemma, an option we regard
as neither possible nor desirable.[3]

In effect, the choice is between war-fighting and the
constabulary principle. We cannot have it all.

Though we must take care to meld existing capabilities acquired under an earlier strategic perspective
into a force structure for the future, the constabulary
principle yields a clear choice. It favours type 1 sovereignty missions, defence of Canadian territory, waters,
and airspace, and international peacekeeping as distinct from forces for warfare and peace enforcement.
In structuring the Canadian Forces for constabulary
action, we would configure and deploy the navy
and air force for the performance of tasks close to
home, whereas the army's capacity to contribute to
international peacekeeping operations would be
enhanced. The government's mission statement for
the Canadian Forces needs to be reduced to two

main points: direct defence of Canada and of type 1 sovereignty, plus aid both to civilian authorities and to the civil power; and international peacekeeping.

As to the first point, activity in support of the defence of Canada and in aid to the state contributes to type 1 sovereignty, and to type 2 sovereignty insofar as the Canadian Forces figure in the national unity process. The defence of Canada includes requirements to exert a military presence at sea, in the air, and on land anywhere within the outer limits of Canadian jurisdiction and perhaps beyond: to conduct surveillance, to identify, and to intercept, and also to deploy force at short notice. Assistance to civilian authorities includes requirements to aid government departments such as Customs and Excise, Human Resources Development, Environment Canada, Fisheries and Oceans, the RCMP, and Transport Canada. Relevant tasks might be drug interdiction, fisheries and environmental surveillance, search and rescue, and disaster relief. Aid to the civil power entails support for the federal government, as in the use of armed force under the War Measures Act, in emergency response to terrorist and related situations, and in support of federal penitentiaries. All considered, defence of Canada and Canadian sovereignty calls for military capabilities fitted to action at the low-intensity end of the scale of armed

violence. Despite some exceptions, naval and air
forces would in practice be oriented to sovereignty
tasks in defence of Canada and in support of civilian
authorities, whereas the army's contribution would
be primarily in aid to the civil power.[4]

Defence of Canada and assistance to civilian
authorities can be provided effectively by a coastal
and territorial defence force. The naval element
could consist of some ten patrol frigates and corvettes
or minor combat vessels, all distributed equally
between the east and west coasts. As to the air force,
it could be composed of four squadrons of eight
CF-18 fighter aircraft each, three surveillance and
search and rescue squadrons, and six tactical and
heavy transport helicopter squadrons, including
those operating off patrol frigates. Forces structured
in this manner could see the sale of Canada's three
submarines and cancellation of the submarine replacement program; storage or sale of some one hundred
CF-18s; storage or sale of the air transport fleet;
termination of patrol and surveillance aircraft update
programs; and closure of a substantial number of
Canada's forty-two military bases and facilities.
When roughly $4 billion annually is spent on infra-
structure and bases alone,[5] it is evident that
substantial savings are to be had from a defence
posture based on the primacy of sovereignty.

As to the second set of activities under the constabulary principle, the army stands to gain a new lease on life with the enhanced importance of international peacekeeping as contrasted to Cold War "collective security" operations in Europe. Depending on the quality and magnitude of peacekeeping capabilities authorized by the government of Canada, the land forces element of the Canadian Forces could consist of a light division comprising three light mobile brigades, one airborne battalion, and various support units totalling roughly 12,000 personnel.[6] Given the standard ratio of 1:2 for forces in the field to those in base and on rotation, there would be some 8,000 army personnel in Canada at any given time. This force would be available to perform tasks in aid to the civil power and in lesser missions including disaster relief and search and rescue. In decisions on the sizing of the land forces, the need to aid the civil power takes precedence in principle over Canadian participation in international peacekeeping activities. In practice, however, the matter is likely to be handled the other way around in view of the abiding wish of Canadians to be internationally active in common security missions.

What, then, would we have by way of national defence if the Canadian Forces were committed primarily to national sovereignty and peacekeeping tasks? Would we not stand dangerously disarmed and needlessly deprived of influence in an uncertain world? In truth, there *is* little defence here in the traditional sense of the term. But we now face an unprecedented situation where the threat of war and the ability to spend are concerned. If we were soon to engage in heavy combat, it would not be to fight alone against a single adversary. But who would our allies be and who our enemies now or in the future? Coalition warfare in Europe is no longer a credible proposition. Something like it is conceivable in the Asia–Pacific region and in the form of peace enforcement as occurred in the war with Iraq. There is also some value in the argument that Canada needs to retain flexible, combat-capable armed forces as backing for effective intervention in economic and diplomatic arenas. But to act on this proposition would be to retain an inadequate force structure intact at a time when credible war-fighting capabilities are well beyond our reach, when change in our external environment gives us new room to act on urgent civil challenges to our security. Whether it be to unite Canadians, to free imagination and energy in addressing a civil security agenda, or to attack specific problems such as the deficit, we have no choice but to reduce our reliance on military means in defending Canada's security and sovereignty.

Though the government has declined to base its armed force requirements on the constabulary principle, the debate is by no means over. Quite the contrary, in dispatching a contingent of only 1,000 troops to support the NATO peace-enforcement mission in Bosnia, Ottawa could be starting to face the realities. Further, the Canadian contingent is to perform tasks that reside very clearly at the low end of the spectrum of violence — mine-clearing, construction, and communications. Add to this the likelihood of a further substantial reduction of defence spending in the 1996 federal budget, and the case for the constabulary principle may yet win the day.

INTELLIGENCE AND PUBLICITY

The country being the size it is, the thought of the Canadian government patrolling effectively against type 1 challenges to sovereignty is not really practical. The RCMP, for example, has reported that only an estimated 10–15 percent of drugs being smuggled into the country was being seized.[7] Whether or not this percentage can be improved upon significantly by more stringent controls at airports and elsewhere, timely intelligence concerning illicit activity is ever more important. Intelligence of this kind can be gathered by electronic means within Canada and in the approaches to the country. It can also be had by human means in Canada and out to the point of origin. Given the high value of intelligence in defence of type 1 sovereignty, Canadian government agencies need to accelerate the creation of an integrated surveillance system for air, sea, and land environments, and for the full range of type 1 challenges.

But who would be responsible for an integrated sovereignty intelligence system in Ottawa? To what extent ought it to be inter-operable with American capabilities, including foreign intelligence-gathering? Moreover, should there not be one place in the federal government where the full range of type 1 and new sovereignty challenges are addressed individually and in their interconnectedness?

Without such a facility, Canada's response to transformations in its international security environment would surely remain unfocused and ineffective. Further, if secrecy in a widening range of security matters is not to add to the distance between state and civil society in Canada, we are in need of greater publicity and public support for efforts being made to strengthen sovereignty.

The better the command, control, communications, and intelligence (C^3I) capabilities we have, the less we need to maintain forces out on patrol, the fewer forces we need, and the less we miss in exercising type 1 sovereignty. As matters stand, the

government of Canada needs to assign high priority
to the development of a C³I surveillance system that
permits near real-time securing of targets on land, in
the air, and out to sea in two and to some extent
three oceans, if we include the Arctic. Steps are in
fact being taken to put a system together,[8] but they
seem unduly casual and fragmentary.

Within the Canadian Forces, Maritime Command has been aware of the need for cooperation
with other government departments, while remain-
ing content to note that "much work remains to be
done."[9] It has also acknowledged an inability to inte-
grate the data generated by the fleets into "a master
C³I network."[10] Meanwhile, a National Acoustic
Centre is planned, as are fixed underwater acoustic
arrays in "locations throughout Canadian maritime
regions."[11] Add to the picture the air forces of various
Canadian government agencies in addition to Air
Command, Canada's recently modernized coastal
radars, the radar and other capabilities associated
with the North Warning System[12] in Canada's Arctic
and with the North American Aerospace Defence
Command (NORAD),[13] and the human intelligence
and other assets of the Canadian Security Intelligence Service (CSIS), and the overall impression can
only be one of disarray, duplication, and cost-
ineffectiveness. All these defects need to be put right.

The Canadian government has to obtain a clear idea of its integrated C³I requirement for the performance of type 1 sovereignty tasks. It needs to put into place the requisite capabilities which, to the degree possible, should be inter-operable with those of the United States. All Canadian electronic data should be fused in a single agency. Rather than create a new body, I suggest that the Communications Security Establishment[14] come in from the cold and be given a mandate to act as central agency for electronic intelligence relating to defence of type 1 sovereignty. CSIS would presumably contribute human intelligence to the pool of knowledge. Control over the total integrated C³I capability for type 1 sovereignty would be vested in the existing Intelligence Advisory Committee in the Privy Council Office.

As regards defence of political sovereignty, the knowledge and science requirements are great and are quite different from those arising with traditional challenges to Canadian sovereignty. A major difference resides in the fact that secrecy is counterproductive in evaluating and acting on type 2 threats. Assessments of Canada's foreign debt and its effects, global warming, or the erosion of Canadian culture should remain a matter of public record. Further, as new sovereignty challenges gain priority in the years ahead, intelligence-gathering by government should become an increasingly open process, with active participation from the private sector. Effective defences of sovereignty, including the readiness to provide requisite funding, are unlikely without widespread public understanding of the dangers we face and of what needs to be done about them.

Accordingly, when scientific and technical considerations loom large in new challenges to sovereignty — for instance, in connection with ozone depletion, new diseases, or technological dependence — the government assessment could be coordinated through the Intelligence Advisory Committee, with expert non-governmental input as required. When the economic and political dimension is uppermost, as with indebtedness or foreign overfishing of straddling stocks in international waters, evaluation could be assigned to relevant government departments that also would consult with the private sector.

To bring the entire effort together, a unit would be created in the Prime Minister's Office. Perhaps called a Common Security Council, this office would advise the prime minister and, otherwise, establish priorities among the varied challenges to Canadian sovereignty and security; seek policy options from government departments; recommend action to Cabinet; and report annually to Parliament and the public on substantive issues of sovereignty facing the country. This office would give forceful expression to an enhanced Canadian capacity for choice in a shrinking world where all players have begun to recognize the critical importance of knowledge in the provision of security.[15] In due course it would put an end to the waste and inadequacy in intelligence-gathering and sovereignty-enforcement. It could also help develop a public understanding of when we are best advised to look after ourselves, and when our purposes are better met in common security action with other countries.

CULTURE AND COMMUNICATIONS

In the early 1950s, it could rightly be said that in defending ourselves we were securing our capacity to make a contribution to civilization. Today, the capacity to contribute to civilization is a precondition for success in defending ourselves against unconventional security threats. The state of our cultural life is now of greater importance than the state of our armed forces in determining our ability to make choices for ourselves in a world where military challenges to our country have diminished relative to non-military or civil dangers. Some people will prefer to regard Canadian culture strictly on its merits. Others will no doubt find it strange to adopt a security perspective on Canadian cultural affairs — one in which culture and communications are viewed in their relationship to autonomy of choice, to issues such as global warming, the acquisition or not of a replacement submarine fleet, and so on. Still, the fact is that Canadian culture and Canadian security have now become closely interconnected. To the degree that funds can be transferred to defence of sovereignty, and away from international security missions that cease to have priority, revenue must go to renewed support for culture and communications.

Though the United States is itself exposed to the effects of globalization, it remains the sharpest threat to the integrity of Canada's cultural life. But we Canadians are ultimately responsible. We have elected governments prepared to diminish civilization in this country, and often we seem not to care about where we're heading. Whether it's the North American logo of Canadian Pacific, a new name for the Canadian Football League, the remarkable rise in the appeal of basketball among Canada's youth, the state of book publishing, the withering of the CBC, the triumph of baseball, and on down a lengthy list, many of us in English-speaking Canada have no problem with the Americanization of Canadian tastes. But we do have a problem insofar as a society that is caring and civil depends upon an indigenous culture and communications process. To awaken Canadians to what's at stake in their cultural life as the millennium approaches, the government ought to establish a new Massey Commission as the first of a series of measures providing an interim response to the erosion of Canadian culture and communications.

Second, and as the Juneau report recommends, the CBC ought to be turned around and allowed to become an authentic public broadcaster again. Bureaucracy, and the separate disabilities of the corporation caused by underfunding, should not hold us back from considering the CBC's potential for renewal and its capacity to voice the Canadian experience. The authors of the Juneau report and others who follow these matters know what needs to be done by way of first steps for the CBC, and for other elements of the cultural sector.[16] But the international security context of cultural renewal is not well known at all. We have the familiar need for Canadian programming in entertainment and information to meet unfamiliar political requirements of autonomous choice in an interdependent world. What we require is a framework of values, ideas, and feelings within which Canadians may express and share their diversity. Such a framework should allow us to view and to discuss *our* reality directly and in symbolic terms — not another country's reality, or that of a homogenized global culture. For the CBC to renew its capacity to draw us together as citizens, not as consumers, political decisions on increased funding are obviously required. Decisions of this kind will require a judgment that deficit-reduction measures cannot be made to stick in a country that is coming apart unless they are offset by renewed support to culture and communications aimed at averting still deeper disunity.

Third, steps should be taken to increase the opportunity for Canadians to see Canadian films in Canada.[17] Some 97 percent of screen time in cinemas in Canada is controlled from the United States as part of the "domestic" American film distribution market. Under NAFTA, it is worth noting, Mexico is able to require that 30 percent of available screen time is held for Mexican films.[18] In Canada, Canadian-made films cannot be screened as they should to Canadian audiences. Nor can film producers readily obtain required funding, owing to the small returns to be had in these circumstances. The government has recently provided tax incentives for film production by replacing the previous capital-cost allowance with tax-credit arrangements which were requested by the industry and which will be compatible with similar provisions already in effect in Quebec.[19] Still other things need to be done to encourage Canadian production of films, such as eliminating the cuts announced in the Telefilm Canada budget in April 1993; and implementing film distribution legislation, prepared as of 1987 but never put forward, to ensure screen time in Canada for Canadian-made films.

Finally, certain measures should be taken to strengthen Canadian publishing. Concessionary postal rates that previously allowed publications to reach the widely dispersed Canadian readership should be reinstated, in the aftermath of incremental reductions that now amount to 70 percent since 1988–89. GST on books, magazines, and newspapers should also be lifted in accordance with traditional exemptions for published materials which remained in force until 1991.

All these things and more we can readily do for ourselves. They can and should be done not to close Canada to the cultural influences of the United States or other countries, but to ensure that the voices of Canadians are heard in Canada. Throughout, the aim should be to underwrite Canada's capacity for choice. This can be achieved by widening the opportunity for Canadians to take part in a common cultural experience and in an interchange of views on their country and the world outside. The more we are knit together, the more civil and caring we are likely to be as a people. The more we view the world through a frame of reference that meets *our* needs, the more effectively we will express ourselves in unilateral action when it is called for, and the more creative we will be in our contribution to common security in concert with others.

As is the case with questions of national defence, the way we deal with cultural issues may already be changing. In January 1996, a Cabinet shuffle brought new hope. Until then and indeed until the Quebec referendum of October 1995, it seemed that the Liberal government, like its Conservative precursor, just did not get it. Still wedded to an industrial and commericial understanding of Canadian civilization, the Liberals seemed unlikely to respond to the Juneau report in particular with a willing commitment to culture and communications in recovering ground for sovereign choice. But with the designation of Shelia Copps as Minister of National Heritage, the outlook of the government seems to have altered. We now have a minister who regards the revitalization of the CBC and other cultural institutions as critical in Canada's "double struggle" with Quebec separatism and Americanization.[20] A double stuggle indeed it is.

NATIONAL UNITY

Two interdependent processes will be at work in the imminent effort to restore a renewed sense of unity in Canada. On the one hand, Quebeckers will make up their own mind as to whether they wish to stay or leave. More important as I see it, Canada, by which I mean very largely the English-speaking population of the country, Aboriginal peoples included, will decide what they want to achieve for an intact or diminished land. Between the two solitudes there will be much signalling and tacit bargaining, and perhaps formal intergovernmental negotiation as well. Canada can be expected this time around to make fully clear the costs of separation to Quebeckers who, for their part, will respond and have messages of their own to send. But each side will ultimately decide for itself in a coordination that leaves much to chance. I think it vital to understand that the decision will depend more on the appeal than on the deprivations each has to offer the other. With English-speaking Canadians being cast in the role of *demandeur* for the Canadian cause, much will depend on our ability to come up with a vision of the country's future that is compelling to us and, secondarily, to the Quebec majority. As with the handling of mutual deprivation, tactical considerations of what will play in Quebec are bound to figure in the design of our aspirations.

We may also be seized by the seeming importance of developments as they unfold in Quebec. But it would be a tragedy if the Canadian side were to become transfixed by the particulars of interaction on constitutional and political relations. As I have been arguing throughout this book, there is no substitute for autonomy of choice — deciding for oneself — for a people who would be sovereign in their space.

English-speaking Canadians must do much more than size up the details of the situation and act accordingly. They must also recover the ground for choice in conceiving a future for Canada that may also have appeal for Quebec. Richard Gwyn has put it as succinctly as anyone: "The country will simply not hold together unless it is animated and sustained by the English-speaking sensibility — outside Quebec."[21]

The situation early in 1996 is one in which Canada ought to cease accommodating Quebec until a new vision and a new architecture have been conceived for the country. As long as the Parti Québécois is in office, concessions and patronage risk being futile and also disabling for those who offer them. Of course there will be exceptions when something of interest in Quebec also makes sense on its merits in Canada, as, for example, with federal regulations governing foreign advertising in magazines.[22] But, in a broad sense, we should stand firm. We should make clear not so much the costs of separation to Quebec, but the benefits *to us* of a Canada that is regaining its sovereignty. Sovereignty, now defined explicitly as the capacity for autonomous choice among English-speaking Canadians, lies at the heart of the effort to make Canada secure.

There is no telling what shape the process will take that sees English-speaking Canada summon the will to renew the country. Grassroots initiatives are springing up all over. The federal Cabinet group on unity has yet to report.[23] Opinion swirls around and then shies away from a two-track approach that would generate public support for dramatic change in the Canadian condition, while also spelling out the terms and consequences of separation, including the rebuilding of Canada if Quebec were to leave.[24] The process and the substance of a new consensus among the population and the regions of English-speaking Canada are obviously of major importance. But everything that has been said in this book points to the still more fundamental need to create enabling preconditions for choice. To deal effectively with a distinct society, English-speaking Canada must re-affirm itself as a distinct society.

Though there is much that can be done to

recover the sense of shared endeavour among English-speaking Canadians in their economic and social life, it is in the celebration of Canadian civilization that common ground from British Columbia to Newfoundland will most readily be found. The government that leads in this area will find itself increasingly popular, even in Quebec. The first test will come in the evolving response to the Juneau report on broadcasting, film, and video in Canada. Let us see that it is passed with flying colours.

VI

Drawing
Together

Even without the separatist movement in Quebec, Canada would be in rough shape today. The sources of our disarray and discontent are many and highly varied. No one needs to be told they run deep. Outwardly manifested in mounting deprivation and cleavages among us, their underlying expression resolves into the decline of sovereignty right down to the individual level. Enhanced sovereignty is the master key to many of the doors that are closed to us now. To find a way through will not be easy in an era of globalization and displacement of the nation-state.

Our task is to escape forward into new avenues of association and well-being. To do so, we will need not only to make sound choices but to create improved conditions for choice itself. Paradoxically, we have no choice in this matter. Everything possible must be done to underwrite Canadian sovereignty in its unconventional political form. The many who would speak for Canada and draw Canadians together must hold Canadian civilization high. Those who would innovate politically must breathe new life into our common culture to provide a better basis for collective decision. Beyond that, the rise of the new sovereignty agenda obliges us to re-evaluate our received understandings of security and our priorities in making Canada secure. What is needed in the end is a sense of the essentials, and of the sequence in which they might be enacted by people and government.

The state of our cultural life and communications towers above all other considerations. Though the impediments to our ability to decide for ourselves on major matters stem from sources larger and more potent than the United States, the fact that the principal challenges to Canadian culture emanate from the United States means in practice that defence of sovereignty requires resistance to American cultural influences in particular. So be it. Measures to revive the CBC, Canadian film and video production, and publishing should be implemented without delay. So should the creation of a royal commission to raise awareness and develop a strategy for cultural survival and adaptation in the next century. In showing a renewed sense of purpose on matters vital to our own continuance, we in English-speaking Canada may also expect to strengthen the appeal in Quebec of a Canada in which they too may continue to live.

Second, the evolution of defence policy must soon yield a reappraisal of Canada's security requirements which conforms to the constabulary principle. As such, it should assign top priority to defence of sovereignty, obviate the need to maintain a substantial capacity for war-fighting, and emphasize participation in international peacekeeping operations that do not entail high levels of coercion. A reappraisal along these lines should in turn follow from a set of capability requirements that is substantially reduced from and more specialized than today's. Further, to meet fully the needs of defence modernization at the turn of the century and beyond, military assistance to civilian authorities and to other government departments should be restructured from top to bottom. Centred on critical functions such as fisheries surveillance and drug interdiction, it should involve *all* relevant government departments, with all fleets and all air forces considered in their interrelationship so as to gain maximum cost-effectiveness.

Third, the machinery of Canadian government needs to be reorganized in order to provide systematic and near real-time intelligence for type 1 sovereignty tasks. This in itself is no small task. It could take years to accomplish unless driven forcibly by political leaders. All government departments with responsibilities bearing on type 1 sovereignty issues should contribute to a centralized C^3I system that is interoperable with U.S. capabilities and is supported by international intelligence cooperation outside North America. Canada–U.S. relations and interests in drug interdiction and related matters being what they are, there should be no problem in cooperating with Washington on C^3I, even as we differ on questions of culture and communications.

Fourth, we need to create in government a process that generates an integrated security perspective which includes type 2 and type 1 sovereignty challenges, as well as peacekeeping, cultural, and other considerations that seem incommensurable under the conventional wisdom. This certainly is a requirement that will be filled only after we've been working at it for a while, and after we've put in place an intelligence-gathering and enforcement capacity for type 1 sovereignty. To begin, however, the precursor to a Common Security Council should be set up in the Prime Minister's Office to start the analytical and policy work of evaluating type 2 sovereignty dangers, of ranking them separately and relative to type 1 problems, and of considering cost-effective common security and unilateral Canadian responses.

Fifth, little or nothing will happen without leadership that gives to the people of English-speaking Canada, and tacitly to Quebeckers, the belief that their views are being considered on the overall direction of Canadian policy. As well as everything else that is on the table, concerned citizens and political leaders must take stock of the transformation in Canada's security situation in the process of renewal that lies ahead. They must speak to the Canadian people about the country's new sovereignty and security requirements, above all the need for support to culture and communications. They must in effect declare a New Sovereignty alert.

Finally, I suggest two benchmarks by which to judge the performance of the Canadian government on behalf of sovereignty in the period ahead. Appropriately enough in view of the emphasis of this book, both have to do with the United States and Canada–U.S. relations. Never mind that the threats to our sovereignty stem from sources wider than those concentrated south of the border, the federal government must find a way to increase the amount of time for Canadian films to be shown on theatre screens in Canada. Whether this can be done by licensing legislation or by other means, the Motion Picture Association of America must recognize the desire of Canadians to recover common ground for choice — to see their own experiences and their own landscapes portrayed on film. Canadians must express their images, thoughts, and feelings more fully to one another, or risk losing their land.

The government should also act on the long-standing commitment to emplace acoustic sensors at key choke points in the waters of the Canadian Arctic Archipelago. If the U.S. navy is found to be using these waters surreptitiously, the government ought to voice its objection. The need to speak out is more urgent now, when the end of the Cold War has reduced U.S. military requirements to use Canadian waters. They have little reason to transit the Archipelago except to add to an international practice consistent with their view of Canada's Arctic waters as an international strait.

Voiceless people do get their land took. If the government of Canada does not show leadership and also speak up on the simple issues of film distribution and Arctic sovereignty, the Canadian people will know they are being taken.

Notes

I / RECOVERING THE GROUND FOR CHOICE

1 Allan R. Gregg, "Can Canada Survive?" *Maclean's*, December 25, 1995/January 1, 1996, 14.
2 Richard Gwyn, *Nationalism without Walls: The Unbearable Lightness of Being Canadian* (Toronto: McClelland & Stewart, 1995). Also of interest are the very different John Ralston Saul, *The Unconscious Civilization* (Toronto: Anansi, 1995), and Linda McQuaig, *Shooting the Hippo: Death by Deficit and Other Canadian Mysteries* (Toronto: Viking, 1995).
3 Canada, Royal Commission on National Development in the Arts, Letters and Sciences, 1949–51, *Report* (Ottawa: Eduard Cloutier, 1951), 274.

II / CANADA'S SECURITY REDEFINED

1 See, for example, Legislative Research Service, Ontario

Legislative Assembly, "Ontario and the 'Four Motors' of Europe," *Current Issue Paper 110* (October 1990), which refers to the agglomerations of economic and political power centred on Barcelona, Lyon, Milan, and Stuttgart in the European Union. See also James Goldsborough, "California's Foreign Policy," *Foreign Affairs* 72 (spring 1993): 88–96.

2 See, for example, Robert Keohane, "Sovereignty, Interdependence and International Institutions," *Working Paper* (Center for International Affairs, Harvard University, spring 1991), 4; or "Speech by the Right Honourable Joe Clark, Secretary of State for External Affairs, to the Vancouver Board of Trade, Vancouver, British Columbia, April 22, 1987," *Statements and Speeches*, External Affairs and International Trade Canada. An excellent review of contemporary problems of sovereignty is to be found in Joseph A. Camilleri and Jim Falk, *The End of Sovereignty? The Politics of a Shrinking and Fragmenting World* (Aldershot: Edward Elgar Publishing, 1992).

3 Elisabeth Mann-Borgese, "Notes on Sovereignty," in The Group of 78, *Beyond Sovereignty: The Future of the Nation State* (Ottawa: Group of 78, 1992), 22–23. See also Barbara McDougall, "Canada and the New Internationalism," *Canadian Foreign Policy* 1 (winter 1992–93): 1–16.

4 In the case of the *Manhattan*, an American supertanker accompanied by a U.S. icebreaker travelled through the Northwest Passage and manoeuvred in its eastern approaches in order to test the potential for shipping Alaskan oil through the Archipelago to markets on the eastern seaboard. Though the tanker conformed to Canadian requirements, the icebreaker neither sought nor obtained permission to enter Canadian waters. The U.S. view, which persists to this day, is that the waterways constituting the Northwest Passage are an international strait and are not sovereign Canadian space. As for the *Polar Sea*, it went through the passage in late summer 1985 without the United States having requested permission, but with permission being granted anyway by an embarrassed

Canadian government. On the *Manhattan* episode, see John
Kirton and Don Munton, "The *Manhattan* Voyages and Their
Aftermath," in Franklyn Griffiths, ed., *Politics of the Northwest
Passage* (Montreal: McGill-Queen's University Press, 1987),
67–97. For the *Polar Sea*, consult Christopher Kirkey,
"Smoothing Troubled Waters: The 1988 Canada–United
States Arctic Co-operation Agreement," *International Journal*
50 (spring 1995): esp. 403–5.

5 "'Their Garden of Eden': Sovereignty and Suffering in
   Canada's High Arctic," *Northern Perspectives* 19 (spring
   1991).

6 The United States experiences an erosion of control over
   their internal affairs that is similar to the effects of globalization as felt by Canadians. Drew Fagan, "Free Trade: The
   Shoe Is on the Other Foot," *Globe and Mail*, November 13,
   1993. See also David E. Rosenbaum, "Beyond a Trade Pact,"
   New York Times, November 11, 1993: "We have seen too
   many jobs lost. We have seen too many families uprooted.
   And we have seen too many communities destroyed in the
   past 12 years" (Representative David E. Senior, Michigan).
   On the growing backlash against globalization, see Thomas
   L. Friedman, "Revolt of the Wannabes," ibid., February 7,
   1996.

7 On the last point, see Shawn McCarthy, "Canadian
   Magazines Imperilled, MPs Warned," *Toronto Star*, October
   20, 1995.

8 William Thorsell, "A New Chapter in the Decline and Fall of
   National Sovereignty," *Globe and Mail*, December 26, 1992.

9 Peter F. Drucker, *Post-Capitalist Society* (New York:
   HarperCollins, 1993), 141–56.

10 See especially John Gerrard Ruggie, "Territoriality and
   Beyond: Problematizing Modernity in International
   Relations," *International Organization* 47 (winter 1993):
   139–74. Also of interest is Stephen D. Krasner, "Compro-
   mising Westphalia," *International Security* 20 (winter
   1995/96): 115–51.

11 The quotation, by Riccardo Petrella, director of science and technology forecasting for the European Community, is from Alvin Toffler and Heidi Toffler, "Societies at Hyper-Speed," *New York Times*, October 31, 1993. Further discussion is available in the Tofflers' *War and Anti-War* (New York: Warner Books, 1993), which breezily refers to a world composed of "thousands of mini-states, city-states, regions and non-contiguous political entities" (289–90).

III / SECURITY AND THE NEW SOVEREIGNTY

1 *Canada 21: Canada and Common Security in the Twenty-First Century* (Toronto: Centre for International Studies, University of Toronto, 1994). An earlier version of this book served as a background document for the Canada 21 project. For opposing views, see Bernard Thillaye, "Thinking about Canadian Defence Policy," *Defence Associations National Network News* 3, No. 2 (August 1995), 12–14; and A. Sean Henry, "Is Canada's Military in for a Bad Year?" *Globe and Mail*, January 5, 1996.

2 Paul Koring, "U.K. Submarines on Horizon," *Globe and Mail*, January 22, 1996.

3 Canada, National Defence, *1994 Defence White Paper* (Ottawa: Supply and Services Canada, 1994), 14.

4 Consider *Canada 21*, and the various discussions in Franklyn Griffiths, "Epilogue: Civility in the Arctic," in Griffiths, ed., *Arctic Alternatives: Civility or Militarism in the Circumpolar North* (Toronto: Science for Peace/Samuel Stevens, 1992), esp. 298–300; Jessica T. Mathews, "Redefining Security," *Foreign Affairs* 69 (1989): 162–77; Ken Booth, "Security and Emancipation," *Review of International Studies* 17 (1991): 313–26; and Simon Dalby, "Security, Modernity, Ecology: The Dilemmas of Post-Cold War Security Discourse," *Alternatives* 17 (1992): 95–134.

5 Canada, *Government Response to the Recommendations of the Special Joint Parliamentary Committee Reviewing Canadian*

Foreign Policy (Ottawa, February 1995), 8, 12, and 21.

6 See the Yablokov report: *Facts and Problems Related to Radioactive Waste Disposal in Seas Adjacent to the Territory of the Russian Federation* (Moscow: Office of the President of the Russian Federation, 1993), which presents the situation in stark detail. We may ask why Ontario Hydro, Hydro-Québec, and Atomic Energy of Canada Ltd. should not join with the government of Canada in an environmental common security venture that would see Canadians contribute to nuclear safety and waste disposal in the Russian and hence Canadian Arctic, and possibly to Canadian unity as well. See also Bill Webb and Mark Cohen, *Competing in the Global Nuclear Industry: Strategic Options for the Canadian Nuclear Industry*, Global Competitiveness Project, Faculty of Management, McGill University, April 1993.

7 Griffiths, "Civility," 288.

8 Public Policy Forum, *Making Government Work* (Ottawa: Public Policy Forum, June 23, 1993).

9 Murray Campbell, "Attitudes on Immigration Harden," *Globe and Mail*, March 10, 1994. Michael Valpy also cites the lack of sufficient Canadian homogeneous tribalness to form national consensus on public policy directions. "Streets: A Fear of Losing the Old Canada," ibid., March 11, 1994.

IV / THREATS TO CANADIAN SOVEREIGNTY

1 Michael Shenstone, "Canadian Immigration Policy and Refugee Policy," in Christopher J. Maule and Fen Osler Hampson, eds., *Canada among Nations 1993–94: Global Jeopardy* (Ottawa: Carleton University Press, 1993), 211–28; and Harold Troper, "Canada's Immigration Policy since 1945," *International Journal* 48 (spring 1993): 255–81.

2 See, for example, Henry Hess, "Some New Citizens Would Shut Door," *Globe and Mail*, October 21, 1993; Jacquie Miller, "Racism Smoulders under Surface of Unspoken 'Immigration' Issue," *Ottawa Citizen*, October 23, 1993; and

Martin Mittelstaedt, "Refugees Accused of Fraud," *Globe and Mail*, October 28, 1993. For comparison, see John Darnton, "Western Europe Is Ending Its Welcome to Immigrants," *New York Times*, August 10, 1993.

3 Shenstone, "Canadian Immigration Policy," 224–28.

4 The outstanding treatment is from Donat Pharand, with Leonard H. Legault, in *The Northwest Passage: Arctic Straits* (Dordrecht: Martins Nijhoff, 1984).

5 Donat Pharand, "Les problèmes de droit international dans l'Arctique," *Revue Etudes internationales* 20 (mars 1989): esp. 158–59.

6 Donald M. McRae, "Arctic Sovereignty: Loss by Dereliction?" *Northern Perspectives* 22, No. 4 (winter 1994–95): 4–9. American nuclear submarines have options other than the Canadian Archipelago in sailing to and from the Arctic Ocean. For a publicized account of a recent voyage, see Abe Dane, "Ice Station X," *Popular Mechanics*, November 1993, 313–14. An editor's note (6) refers to the route as "a secret under-ice passageway," which could have been the international waterway through Nares Strait between Ellesmere Island and Greenland.

7 Paul Koring, "Collenette Drops Plan to Monitor Arctic," *Globe and Mail*, February 3, 1996. See also the op-ed comment by Terry Fenge, "Submarines and Arctic Sovereignty," ibid., February 10, 1996. The letter just cited is dated, appropriately enough, May 24, 1995, to the author from Randall McCauley, senior adviser, Office of the Minister of National Defence. If cost considerations alone were the problem, Canada could well seek to buy or even rent the necessary equipment from the Russians who suffer from an overabundance of military hardware and a big need for hard currency.

8 There is a choice here: Was the crash of the northern cod stock off Newfoundland the result of illegal foreign fishing inside Canada's 200-mile fisheries zone, of foreign fishing of straddling stocks in international waters, of Canadian overfishing in Canadian waters, of marine climate change, of all of

the above? In my estimate, the problem is primarily environmental. See Max Dunbar, "Why Have the Cod Gone? It's Just Too Cold Down There," *Globe and Mail*, August 17, 1993. It has in any case been addressed by the Canadian government at the United Nations Conference on High Seas Fishing. Accordingly, I regard it as a type 2 sovereignty problem.

9 See Lydia Dotto, "Global Warming: Dealing with Uncertainty," ibid., November 13, 1993, and William K. Stevens, "Scientists Say Earth's Warming Could Set Off Wide Disruptions," *New York Times*, September 18, 1995, on the dilemmas of choice in response to global warming. On ozone depletion as a heightened threat, see Geoffrey York, "Animals, Forests and Fish Threatened by Ultraviolet-B," ibid.; and John Noble Wilford, "Antarctic Ozone Hits Record Low," *New York Times*, October 19, 1993.

10 Gwyn, *Nationalism without Walls*, 16.

11 Camilleri and Falk, *End of Sovereignty*, esp. 83, 88, and 243, provides a basis for the reflections that follow.

12 Data in this paragraph are derived largely from work by Paul Audley, to whom a debt is acknowledged. See his "Cultural Industries Policy: Objectives, Formulation and Evolution," a paper prepared December 1992 for the Social Sciences and Humanities Research Council of Canada and the federal Department of Communi-cations; and *The Arts and Artists in Ontario in the Context of the Cultural Sector and Cultural Policy* (Toronto: Culture and Communications Ontario, May 1992). Also relevant are an advertisement, "Without Glue Nations Come Unstuck," *Globe and Mail*, October 20, 1993, C3; and *Vital Links: Canadian Cultural Industrial Policy* (Ottawa: Department of Communications/Supply and Services Canada, April 1987).

13 Christopher Harris, "Cuts Will Sap CBC, Group Warns," *Globe and Mail*, December 6, 1995; and Michael Valpy, "The Beleagured CBC and the Delayed Juneau Report," ibid., January 16, 1996.

14 Audley, *Arts and Artists*, 22–23.

15 Mandate Review Committee — CBC, NFB, Telefilm, *Making Our Voices Heard: Canadian Broadcasting and Film for the 21st Century* (Ottawa: Supply and Services, 1996). See also Hugh Winsor and Michael Valpy, "Cable, Phone Tax Urged for CBC," *Globe and Mail*, January 18, 1996; Hugh Winsor, "Cable Industry Vows to Fight," ibid., January 19, 1996; and Robert Fulford, "The Television Taste Test: Is It Private or CBC?", ibid., February 6, 1996.
16 William Thorsell, "The Marketplace Bends to the Knee of Consumer Sovereignty," ibid., November 18, 1995.

V / WHAT IS TO BE DONE?

1 Canada. Department of National Defence, *1995–96 Estimates, Part III: Expenditure Plan* (Ottawa: Supply and Services Canada, 1995), 16.
2 Ibid.
3 *Canada 21*, 63. See also Douglas Bland, "A Strategy of Choice: Preparing the Canadian Armed Forces for the 21st Century," *Canadian Foreign Policy* 2 (spring 1994): 109–36.
4 DND reports as follows on support to other government departments for fiscal year 1992–93: for fisheries surveillance, assistance to Fisheries and Oceans consisted of eighty ship days costing an estimated $18,215,444 plus 1,088 aircraft hours at $12,525,423; for drug interdiction, support to the RCMP came to fifty-eight ship days costing $13,206,197 and 2,374 aircraft hours at $22,635,801; for environmental surveillance in support of the Department of the Environment, 161.5 dedicated flying hours at $561,748 plus 1,560 sea days and 2,526 flying hours as secondary task costing $38,428,000, calculated as 10 percent of total cost. In the case of environmental surveillance, nineteen incidents were reported in 1992–93. Costs include all personnel costs, all related fixed and variable operations and maintenance costs, and allocated costs such as depreciation. Source: letter to author dated November 17, 1993, from N.M. Wildgoose,

director general, Policy Coordination, DND. The combined
cost of support to other departments for fisheries surveillance, drug interdiction, and environmental protection thus
came to $105,572,613.00 in 1992–93, when the total
defence budget was $12.4 billion. Other relevant informa-
tion supplied by DND is as follows: sovereignty patrols,
aircraft hours classified, 3,197 person hours ($712,635);
search and rescue, 104 ship hours ($986,670) and 4,332 air-
craft hours ($21,849,486); disaster relief, thirty-eight person
days ($8,470) and 378 flying hours ($460,282); support to
federal penitentiaries, 150 person days ($33,436); and
ground searches, 270 person days ($60,185). I wish to thank
officials in the Department of National Defence for their
assistance and indeed diligence in generating the information presented here.

5 C.M. Thomas (former vice-chief of the Defence Staff),
"Canadian Defence — 1993 and Beyond," *Defence
Associations National Network News 2* (April 1993): 10. Note
also that some $900 million is spent annually to maintain
Canada's reserve force of 29,000. *1995–96 Estimates*, 169
and 173.

6 Here and in much of the detail on naval and air forces
required for defence of sovereignty, I am drawing upon
Bland, "Strategy of Choice," a paper originally prepared for
the Canada 21 project.

7 See André Picard, "Drug Smugglers Going for Big Score,"
Globe and Mail, November 20, 1993. As of November 1993,
annual seizures of heroin and cocaine were, respectively,
140.5 and 2,028 kilograms. The reported estimate of the
RCMP on cocaine flow into Canada in 1991 is that 86 percent was moved in by air, 22 percent by sea, and 12 percent
by land. In the United States drug interdiction has been losing favour to a "kingpin" strategy employing informers and
other means to take out leading traffickers. Joseph B.
Treaster, "U.S. Altering Tactics in Drug War," *New York*

Times, September 17, 1993; and Michael deCourcy Hinds, "Center for Drug Intelligence Opens, but Some Ask If It Is Really Needed," ibid., November 17, 1993.

8 See Vice-Admiral Peter W. Cairns, "On Course for the Future: Canada's Maritime Forces in the Post Cold-War Era," *Canadian Defence Quarterly* 22 (spring 1993): 8 and 10; and Department of Maritime Command, *The Maritime Command Vision: Charting the Course to Navy 2008* (Ottawa: National Defence, 1993), 2–7.

9 *Maritime Command Vision*, 3–5.

10 Ibid., 2–7.

11 Ibid., 2–5.

12 The North Warning System (NWS) is a joint Canadian–U.S. air defence radar line to warn against a Russian strategic bomber and cruise-missile attack on North America. Along with much else, it is vulnerable to elimination in defence reappraisals in both Canada and the United States. In 1993–94, a total of thirty-six unattended gap-filling radars were installed by the United States to complete the line, which otherwise would have had significant gaps. Even then, the NWS is problematic. Incoming aircraft, unless they happen to pass near a Canadian forward operating location in the Arctic with CF-18s present, are in and out of the detection area before an interceptor can be brought to locate and otherwise deal with the intruder. It is also the case that the NWS was designed against bombers flying at altitude; it is not so effective against low-flying aircraft such as the Rockwell Air Commander, which is favoured by drug runners for long-distance runs. The NWS thus has only little value as a detection system for drug interdiction purposes. Annual operating costs, shared by Canada and the United States, on a 40:60 basis, are currently $97 million to Canada. *1995–96 Estimates*, 128. In fiscal 1992–93, the NWS reported only fifty-six unauthorized tracks in or near Canada, most of which were identified once

planes had landed and notified Transport Canada. Source: see note 4 in this chapter. In cooperation with the U.S. government, the NWS could well be mothballed; the same applies to NORAD.

13 As with U. S. nuclear attack submarines being employed for environmental research, NORAD has for some time been on the lookout for new missions to remain relevant in changing times. See Eric Schmitt, "Colorado Bunker Built for Cold War Shifts Focus to Drug Battle," *New York Times*, July 18, 1993. On the U.S. Navy, see "Arctic Research: The Cold War Chills Out," *Science* 261 (July 2, 1993): 26.

14 The Communications Security Establishment reports to Parliament through the minister of national defence. With a budget estimated at $240 million, it concentrated for many years on the collection of intelligence on Soviet military activity by eavesdropping on radio communication from Alert on Ellesmere Island. The CSE is no doubt acquiring other missions now, but still produces intelligence on Russia. On the domestic operations of the CBC, see Estanislao Oziewicz, "Watchdog Planned for Spy Agency," *Globe and Mail*, January 26, 1996.

15 Broadly analogous proposals were advanced in the *Canada 21* report, 75, and in the 1994 parliamentary review of foreign policy. The government response was confined to the establishment of a global issues office in DFAIT. Canada, *Government Response*, 8.

16 *Making Our Voices Heard.* See also "Without Glue Nations Come Unstuck," and Audley, "Cultural Policy," and *Arts and Artists*.

17 Film and TV Council of Canada, *Press Release*, October 5, 1993.

18 Film and TV Council of Canada, *Press Conference Documents*, October 5, 1993.

19 Winsor, "Cable Industry Vows to Fight."

20 Ray Conlogue and Val Ross, "Arts Community Welcomes

Copps to New Portfolio," *Globe and Mail*, January 26, 1996, and Hugh Winsor, "Copps Backs Spirit of Juneau's CBC Report," ibid., February 1, 1996.

21 Gwyn, *Nationalism without Walls*, 282.

22 McCarthy, "Canadian Magazines Imperilled, MPs Warned." The reference here is to the threat faced by French-language publications in Quebec from split-run editions of European magazines.

23 Susan Delacourt, "Massé Admits Situation 'Urgent,'" *Globe and Mail*, January 19, 1996.

24 Delacourt, "Spicer Plan Sets Timetable for Votes on Unity," ibid., January 18, 1996; "Charest Condemns Secession Planning," ibid., January 20, 1996; and "Tough Talk Deleted from Federalist Script," ibid., February 7, 1996.